Somewhere in Southern Indiana

Poems of Midwestern Origins

Books by
NORBERT KRAPF

Poetry (limited editions)

  The Playfair Book of Hours   (1976)
  Arriving on Paumanok   (1979)
  Lines Drawn from Dürer   (1981)
  Heartwood   (1983)
  Circus Songs   (1984)
  A Dream of Plum Blossoms   (1985)
  East of New York City   (1986)
  March Songs for an English Half-Moon   (1988)

Translator/Editor

  Beneath the Cherry Sapling: Legends from Franconia   (1988)
  Shadows on the Sundial: Selected Early Poems of Rainer
    Maria Rilke   (1990)

Editor

  Finding the Grain: Pioneer Journals, Franconian Folktales,
    Ancestral Poems   (1977)
  Under Open Sky: Poets on William Cullen Bryant   (1986)

SOMEWHERE IN SOUTHERN INDIANA

Poems of Midwestern Origins

by Norbert Krapf

TIME BEING BOOKS
POETRY IN SIGHT AND SOUND
Saint Louis, Missouri

Time Being Books
10411 Clayton Road
Saint Louis, Missouri 63131

Time Being Books volumes are printed on acid-free paper, and binding materials are chosen for strength and durability.

ISBN 1-877770-89-2
ISBN 1-877770-90-6 (pbk.)
ISBN 1-877770-91-4 (tape)

Library of Congress Cataloging-in-Publication Data

Krapf, Norbert, 1943-
 Somewhere in southern Indiana: poems of midwestern origins / by Norbert Krapf. — 1st ed.
  p. cm.
  ISBN 1-877770-89-2 (HC): $16.95. — ISBN 1-877770-90-6 (PB): $9.95. — ISBN 1-877770-91-4 (tape): $9.95
  1. German Americans — Indiana — Poetry. 2. Middle West — Poetry. I. Title.
PS3561.R27S58 1993   93-14729
811'.54 — dc20   CIP

Manufactured in the United States of America

First Edition, first printing (April 1993)

Acknowledgments

Some of these poems originally appeared in the following publications, often in different form: *American Scholar* ("For an Old Friend"); *Arete* ("Curving Back"); *Beanfeast* ("Cutting Wood: After a Family Photograph"); *Blueline* ("Uncle"); *Blue Unicorn* ("Southern Indiana"); *Calliope* ("The Patoka River and the Blessinger Brothers"); *Confrontation* ("Pin Oak" and "To Obscure Men"); *Images* ("Hills," "Hoosier Songs," "My Father Young Again," and "Purple Trillium"); *Kansas Quarterly* ("Darkness Comes to the Woods" and "Flight"); *New Proteus* ("Remembering Heavy Snows"); *North Atlantic Review* ("Theodore Dreiser's Cathedral"); *Old Hickory Review* ("Sugar Maple"); *Poetry Now* ("Basketball Season Begins," "Butchering: After a Family Photograph," "Somewhere in Southern Indiana," and "The Woods of Southern Indiana"); *Raccoon* ("Indigo Bunting"); *Studies in Indiana German-Americana* ("German Fries"); *Western Humanities Review* ("Skinning a Rabbit"); and *West Hills Review* ("A Postcard from Missouri" and "Sisters").

"A Union Veteran from Indiana Recalls Visiting with Walt Whitman in a Washington Hospital" originally appeared in *Paumanok Rising* (Street Press, 1981), edited by Vince Clemente and Graham Everett, and "Boy Scouts Camping Out" in *The Sound of a Few Leaves* (Rook Press, 1977), edited by Cis and Ernie Stefanik.

"Shooting a Squirrel" was originally published as a pamphlet in England by the Sceptre Press (1974). "Squirrel at the Birdfeeder" and "Walnut" first appeared as broadsides in the Stone House Press Broadside Series, "The Forefather Arrives" appeared first as a Rook Press broadside (1976), and "A Pioneer Wedding" was issued as a Kirby's Corners Press pamphlet (1979). A number of the poems appeared in the limited editions *Arriving on Paumanok* (Street Press, 1979), *Heartwood* (Stone House Press, 1983), and *A Dream of Plum Blossoms* (Sparrow Press, 1985) and in the author's *Finding the Grain: Pioneer Journals, Franconian Folktales, Ancestral Poems* (Dubois County Historical Society, 1977); and two poems were reprinted in *The Space Between: Poets from Notre Dame, 1950-1991* (University of Notre Dame Press, 1991), edited by James Walton.

Thanks to the editors of all these publications, especially Graham Everett, Morris Gelfand, and Felix Stefanile, for giving many of these poems a previous life. The author wishes to express his gratitude to the trustees of Long Island University for the 1991-92 sabbatical and to the C.W. Post research committee of Long Island University for the released time which helped make the completion of this volume possible.

Special thanks to Grace Volick for her steadfast encouragement and support and to Lori Loesche, Sheri Vandermolen, and Jerry Call of Time Being Books for the skills they contributed to the development of this book.

*For my mother, Dorothy Schmitt Krapf,
in memory of my father, Clarence Alphonse Krapf,*

*and with thanks to my Hoosier schoolmaster,
Jack London Leas*

Every time a man journeys out into life he is accompanied by a good angel who has been bestowed upon him in the guise of an intimate companion. He who does not sense the good fortune that this companion brings him will nevertheless feel a sore loss the minute he crosses the border leading from his fatherland, where the angel will then forsake him. This benevolent companion is none other than the inexhaustible store of tales, legends, and history, all of which coexist and strive to bring us closer to the refreshing and invigorating spirit of earlier ages.

— The Brothers Grimm
translated by Robert Ward

For song, issuing from its birth-place, after fulfillment, wandering,
Reck'd or unreck'd, duly with love returns.

— Walt Whitman

Contents

Part One: THE FOREFATHER ARRIVES

The Forefather Arrives   19
Entering the Southern Indiana Wilderness   20
Jasper: The Foundation   21
A Pioneer Wedding   22
The Pigeons of St. Henry, Indiana   24
Butchering: After a Family Photograph   25
Tillie, Josie, and Marie   26
Uncle   29
A Postcard from Missouri   32

Part Two: THE WOODS OF SOUTHERN INDIANA

Cutting Wood: After a Family Photograph   37
The Woods of Southern Indiana   39
Remembering Heavy Snows   40
Shooting a Squirrel   42
Squirrel at the Birdfeeder   43
Indigo Bunting   45
Sweet Gum   46
Pin Oak   47
Shagbark Hickory   48
Chamomile   49
Purple Trillium   50
Tulip Poplar   52
Pawpaw   53
Persimmon   54
Dutchman's Breeches   55
Sugar Maple   56
Walnut   57

Skinning a Rabbit   58
Driving Back Roads Late at Night   60
Darkness Comes to the Woods   61
Southern Indiana   62

Part Three: CURVING BACK

Hoosier Songs   67
St. Meinrad Archabbey   68
To Obscure Men   69
Two Bricks and a Board   70
My Father Young Again   75
A Terre Haute Story   79
German Fries   81
Sisters   83
A Civil War Veteran from Indiana Recalls Visiting
      with Walt Whitman in a Washington Hospital   84
Theodore Dreiser's Cathedral   87
Flight   93
Boy Scouts Camping Out   94
The Patoka River and the Blessinger Brothers   95
For an Old Friend   97
Basketball Season Begins   98
Hills   99
Curving Back   101
Somewhere in Southern Indiana   106

SOMEWHERE IN SOUTHERN INDIANA

Poems of Midwestern Origins

Part One:
THE FOREFATHER ARRIVES

* This symbol is used to indicate that a stanza has been divided because of pagination.

The Forefather Arrives

He stumbles off the ship *America*,
parts from the people who
speak the only tongue he's
ever known, and leads a wife
and six children toward the middle
of a dark continent. Eight
pairs of shoes shaped
by the contours of cobbled
Bavarian streets must soon
begin to fall evenly upon
uncultivated ground. Like
a startled rabbit, the woman
cocks her ears for the pealing
of distant church bells.
The children cling to the man's
overcoat like cockleburrs.
A sailor whose eyes blink
back to the vineyards patching
the banks of the Main River,
he knows he must learn to
navigate this foreign land
by foot. He stares at the bark
of trees he's never seen,
flinches at the songs
of birds he's never heard.
He worries about laying seed
in the soil in the spring.
He sucks in his breath,
puts down one foot at a time.

Entering the Southern Indiana Wilderness

As they prepare to step on land,
the Ohio River swirls and heaves
darkly beneath them. Soon he
and his family try to tread
hilly terrain flooded in shade.
No Franconian sunlight lifts
them to buoyancy. Hazy leaves
spindling at the top of sycamore
and tulip poplar seven feet thick
float one hundred fifty feet
above his head. Even at noon
he feels sunk in twilight.
Like a fish channeled into
a strange sea, he quivers along
a trail the buffalo had drummed
onto the forest floor. Deer paths
intersect the trail, then slither
like water moccasins into the darkness.
He runs his fingertips along
the gashes the black bear
clawed like a foreign alphabet
into the bark of sugar maples.
He observes the hills and streams
sloping southwesterly back toward
the Ohio. He feels he is swimming
upstream, toward an alien source.

Jasper: The Foundation

Where an Indian trail crossed Patoka River,
where Benjamin Enlow had built his mill

south of the Trace the buffalo hoofs
had drummed onto the forest floor

Scots and Irish Presbyterians laid out
a town: 102 acres of thick forest.

County commissioners wanted to name it
"Eleanor," after the miller's wife.

She said *No*, opened the Bible to Revelations
and read of the Heavenly City: *And the*

*foundations of the wall of the city were
adorned with all manner of precious stones.*

The first foundation was Jasper. Twelve Catholic
families from Baden soon trudged the mud streets.

A Pioneer Wedding

I. The Invitation

It was the fall of 1854
and brother Johann Krapf,
almost bursting the brass
buttons of the Bavarian suit
he had packed in a trunk,
mounted a horse in the barnyard.
In his right hand he held
like a lance the white oak
staff his father Michael
carved with an heirloom knife.
Like a knight from Franconia,
Johann galloped away down
the hill holding the white staff
high in the rays of September
sun slashing through the forest.
Whenever he approached a farmhouse
in a clearing, he lowered the staff,
rapped at the door, cleared his
throat, and cried out in his best
Franconian dialect: *My sister
is getting married on the 26th.
Please come*. Every neighbor tied
a colored ribbon to the staff.
When Johann galloped back up
the hill, Michael stood squinting
at the rainbow of ribbons rippling
in the sun. He waved, thought
of the wife buried under a tombstone
in a field in Lower Franconia.

II. The Wedding Day — September 26, 1854

Ja, said Elisabeth. *Ja*, said John.
As the bride and groom kissed
at the altar of St. Ferdinand's Church,
named after the emperor, brother
Johann filled out his brocaded
Bavarian suit. He could feel
the eyes of his sweetheart Theresia
warming his back. The white-haired
father of the bride, Michael, stood
to the side daydreaming of a wedding
in the Hesslar Kirche. The organ
rolled like the Atlantic; they proceeded
down the aisle, ducked a storm
of raining grains, and flinched
as shotguns boomed. A wagon
bounced them over the corduroy
road to the brick farmhouse
on a hill just over the Spencer
County line. A hog was roasting
on the spit. Neighbors gathered
in the clearing, clanked mugs
of beer, sang in the old tongue,
and danced as fiddles played.
Schnapps flowed. Johann puffed out
his cheeks as if he were a tuba.
Theresia giggled. Elisabeth smiled.
She lifted her long white dress
and waltzed across the southern
Indiana earth with her husband.
She walked through the crowd,
gave a ring-heavy hand to her
father, and drew him into
the center of the clearing. He
smiled, followed wherever she led.

The Pigeons of St. Henry, Indiana

In God's groves of white oaks
on the hills of the farms
of Edele, Schwoeppe, and Jochum
outside the village
of St. Henry, Indiana

the huge pigeons flapped
down from a darkening sky
& roosted so thickly
limbs could be heard
cracking in the night
like thunderclaps
& crashing to the ground.

Mornings the German Catholics
woke up & walked knee-deep
in all the pigeon
they could eat or sell.

Sometimes in season
they swabbed the earth
around the base
of the great oaks
with corn mash
cooked in kettles

came back & found
wobbly birds
they picked up
by the hundreds.

The going price
of pigeons
was 25 cents a bushel,
delivered.

They all went.

Butchering: After a Family Photograph

(in memory of my grandmother,
Mary Hoffman Schmitt, 1883-1979)

In front of the weathered smokehouse
the scaled hogs hang, hind feet
tied to an ash sapling wedged
between forks in the framing maples.
The squeals of animals dying have
long since frozen into silence.
Snouts have dripped circles of blood
onto a sheet of January snow.
In a field behind the smokehouse
(out of range of the camera eye)
the women empty intestines thin
as onion skin for casings while
other innards boil in iron pots.
Carving at a carcass in the middle
of the picture, the men half turn
and frown as if to say: "We kill
to survive. Starvation lurks just
down the road. We have no time
for your art or your sentimentality."
The man in overalls and boots who
squints the hardest is my grandfather,
thirty-three. Three years later,
on doctor's advice, he took a walk.
Zero-degree breezes fanned the flames
of consumption hidden in his chest.
Two weeks later he lay in cold earth.

Tillie, Josie, and Marie

A gravel lane off the ribbed
rockroad wound between hills
to a sandy barnyard where
skinny brother and pale sister
lived in a farmhouse, once
a log cabin, with a heavyset
mother who never learned
to speak English.

Great-Aunt Tillie never
let German stand in the way
of communicating with the oldest
son of a favorite nephew.
I would nod and smile
as if I understood all
or look to my father
for quick translation.

German was the coin
of Aunt Tillie's realm.

She smiled at the door
as I stood with my father,
shotgun on shoulder, waiting
to plunge into the woods
to hunt the fox squirrels
that would back around
the trunk of a hickory
as an eager boy circled
the trunk below peering
for a glimpse of the red fur
in which to bury the shiny
bead on his gun barrel.

Before we returned from
her woods, Tillie dug up
a clump of rare white lilies
from the edge of her vegetable
garden and wrapped them
in moist burlap for Mother.

Marie, hair tied back tight
in a bun, hovered like
a hummingbird in the kitchen
whenever we visited. I never
saw her stand still, rarely
got to hear the delicate notes
of her infrequent song.

Brother Josie, scrawny frame
pressed against the outline
of his overalls, grinned
a hello and rushed for
the barn with a face always
a little too sunburned.

When Aunt Tillie died,
they laid her out
in a plain wood coffin
in the living room.
I stood in the pool
of silence and stared
at her thick, frozen lips
wondering where all her
earthy German words had gone.

Only they could summon her back.

When Josie died years later,
they found jugs of wine
and bottles of moonshine
stashed in the fields he plowed
and the sheds he tended.
Even in the worst of winters
he never lost his sunburn.

Marie wrote the perfect
script and score for her
quiet death. As she sat
playing the organ in the choir
loft of St. Henry Church at Sunday
*

High Mass, her heart collapsed
and she slumped over. Morning
sunlight slanting through
the base of the stained-glass
window at her side illuminated
the names of her grandparents.

Uncle

After his wife
of a lifetime
died of cancer

he sat alone
at night
in the farmhouse

listening to the
Grand Ole Opry
pulse on the radio

reading the daily
local line by line
front to back

& puffing his
face with popcorn
that raised the lid

off the iron pot
squatting on blue
flame on the stove.

Sometimes when winds
stopped scraping
dried catalpa leaves

in the barnyard
he would whisper
one name to

dull walls:
Elizabeth,
    Elizabeth.

        * * *

Daughters-in-law
sent pots of soup
with the sons

who careened down
the rockroad in pickups
to milk the herd

of bawling cows.
Case tractors
wheeled by sons

& grandsons cut
O's & X's
in the mud between

granary & silo
as coon hounds dozed
beneath the walnut.

    * * *

When a woman
from the other
side of the county

whose husband had
died became his
late bride

& moved into
the farmhouse where
my mother had slept

as a girl squinting
through cracks
in the roof

at snowflakes
& starlight,
frowns caked

the faces of
my cousins.
There was one

name they would
not voice on
the farm they

felt was theirs:
Margaret,
            Margaret.

A Postcard from Missouri

It is a sepia photograph
of three pretty women sitting
in front of a wild rosebush
in bloom. A picket fence
comes to a corner behind their
backs. Except for the familiar
Bavarian bulb of their noses,
I would not recognize them.
Their wide-brimmed straw hats
recline on their laps, their
hair is parted in the middle
and pulled back. Their flowing
dresses cover knees, legs,
and feet, push up their waists,
enclose their necks with
embroidery. You could almost
expect Huck Finn and Tom Sawyer
to pop up behind the fence
and give you the razzberry.

The sleeves of the young woman
in the middle are pulled back
to her elbows, her hands perch
just below her elevated waist.
Just look at me! her squinting
eyes and slightly pursed
lips seem to say, *See how
I've blossomed like this bush!*
On the back of the snapshot
she glued a 1-cent stamp postmarked
Glennonville, Mo., June 25, 1919,
and addressed it to *Mr. and Mrs.
Benno Krapf / St. Henry / Ind.,*
my grandfather and grandmother.

I recall my father's story
about the day his uncle pulled
up to the house with his wife,
*

children, and belongings packed
in a wagon. The two brothers
drank a beer and said good-bye.
My grandfather told his brother
he was crazy. My great-uncle
snapped the reins, and they
lurched toward the West.

Dear Uncle and Aunt, wrote
the pretty girl in front
of the wild rosebush in bloom,
*Well, how are you all getting
along and how are you, hope
all well as we are at present.*
No wonder the lady on the left
is giving the girl posed in
the middle such a horsey grin!
*We have so much work to do,
and it rains so much here lately
we can't do much the last few days.*
No wonder that rosebush
is in such luxuriant bloom!
*Plowing corn is about all,
Will Close With Love / Celia.*

Ah, Celia, it would've been
such fun to meet you. I'd have
plowed corn with you any day!

Part Two:
THE WOODS OF
SOUTHERN INDIANA

Cutting Wood: After a Family Photograph

(in memory of my father)

The steam engine clatters
in a frosted hollow of southern
Indiana hills. White puffs of steam
hang above a hedgerow of bare trees
in the background. You stand there,
grandfather, the ends of your moustache
curling about the corners of unsmiling
lips, gazing at the circular saw about
to bite into the green pulp of a log.
I feel in my blood your reverence
for the medium of wood, respect
your demand for the precise cut.

For twenty-five years your son
crafted processed wood into chairs.
He often stared at the grains
in woods. Now I, who remember
touching your hand only once before
you died in my third year, sit behind
a desk and daydream of the forests
that fed your saw. Soon after you
lay in the earth, your son led me
into the woods and cupped my ears
to the leafy murmurs of shagbark hickory,
wild cherry, oak and beech. He taught
me how to kill for food the animals
that fed on the fruits of those trees.

One summer's work in a wood factory
still has me running my fingertips
over the finished grains of woods
your rough saw once cut into lumber.
With your love of the precise cut,
grandfather, you would understand
my need to carve with a pen
a line smooth and delicate as wild
*

cherry, yet tough and durable
as hickory. I glide over sawdust
toward you, with the shadow
of the anonymous photographer
caught in his picture.

The Woods of Southern Indiana

The woods of southern Indiana
are filled with wild animals
that roam all night. When lights
go out in farmhouses, they creep
out of woods, explore barnyards,
sniff garbage cans, raid chicken
pens, drift back into the hills
at the first hint of light.

When I moved away from southern
Indiana, a part of me broke loose
and joined those wild animals.
No one has ever been able to
track me down. Once in a while
a night hunter will catch a glimpse
of my eyes when he flashes his
light in the branches of a beech.
Every farmer seems to have one
hound in his barnyard that barks
one dark night a year, then curls
up and sleeps through the day.
Whenever the Patoka River floods
the bottom lands, then drains,
my tracks have been found caked
in the mud between rows of corn.

Once when I returned to the scenes
of my youth, I walked deep into
the forest, stood beneath a shagbark
hickory from which I had shot squirrels,
saw several branches bend, and tingled
as a speck of fur flew from the tree.

Sometimes reading my own poems late
at night, I seem to perceive tracks
of my former self between my darkest
lines, but I have never been able
to match the feet that carried
me here with the prints I detect there.

Remembering Heavy Snows

When I opened my eyes
to the whiteness sparkling
on the branches outside
the bedroom window and watched
it swirl across the backyard
against the maple trees like
a trace of the glacier I'd
read about in a geography book,
I knew there was no school.

Soon with breakfast steaming
in my gut and a bolt-action
.22 rifle resting on my
well-insulated shoulder,
I crunched through the snow
into the woods where small
tracks from the night before
led me to kick brushpile after
brushpile to jump a cottontail.

By noon with all that wet
snow bending the hundreds
of intersecting branches above
my head and almost engulfing
my rubber boots, I found
myself in a prehistoric
snow forest tracking mammoth
web-footed creatures never
seen by another human.

Later in the afternoon
with the darkness settling
early upon crusting snow,
I returned empty-handed
but overflowing like someone
who has visited an ancient
world nobody else even
suspects of still existing.

And today, today when
the first snow falls later
and lighter each winter
and scientists tell us
the coniferous forest
has been creeping farther
north into the tundra

I think back to the wet
snow falling silently
in the darkness outside
that faraway bedroom where
I slept as a boy and sometimes
discover myself the accidental
survivor of a time almost
beyond my capacity to recall.

Shooting a Squirrel

I squeezed the trigger:
   a squirrel crashed
     on its belly
at my feet
   and clawed
     the forest floor.

Staring into its
   fading eyes
     I felt myself
tumbling down a tunnel
   into a pit
     where bodies sprawled.

Even today, sometimes
   I sidestep
     manhole covers
swerve past
   subway entrances
     fidget on
       elevators.

Squirrel at the Birdfeeder

When I flap up the kitchen shades
he stares, fat-cheeked, from the bird-
feeder swaying in the gnarled lilac.

Defender of birds' rights,
I rap at the cold pane
dividing my kingdom from his

and aim a fist at his head.
He rises on haunches, fluffs
a tail at my face, wobbles

into the woodpile. . . . As evening
tilts down the hillside, I stray
from a novel propped on the table

and watch sparrows peck seed.
A streak of fur attacks the lilac,
flushing wings into the dusk.

He squeezes onto the ledge
where seed spills from the mouth
of the cave. He gorges as

I swirl from the table like
a storm, cocks ears as I
blast through the doorway,

and freezes as I shake a fist
and gesture like a priest who
can't believe his own sermon.

Since no buckshot has ever spread
from my fingertips, since seed will
spill from the lilac bush again

in the morning, he chews, listens,
chews, backs away when I come
almost close enough to touch.

➜

He hops to a rock, claws bark
to the bottom branch of a locust. . . .
Rocking back and forth in the kitchen,

I think of him poised in the locust,
drift into a forest where branches
give beneath the advance of squirrels.

Indigo Bunting

Back when I was
as convinced as only
a young skeptic can be

that I would never meet
anyone to fall in love with

would never wake up
between warm sheets
breathing in unison
with the right woman

would certainly never marry

couldn't conceivably know
the pleasure of looking
deep into the eyes
of a son or daughter

I was walking alone
along a winding rockroad
in my beloved hills
of southern Indiana.

I was kicking rocks
with my right foot
into dry Queen Anne's lace
in the hot August sun.

A faint whir skimmed
across those flat
tops of snowy white.

I looked up just in time

to see a streak of blue
so pure and sweet
I thought I had never
looked up at the sky.

For the first time,
my friend, I was
ashamed of my certainty.

This blue is for you.

Sweet Gum

In the fall red
star-shaped leaves
visible from afar
to anyone journeying
through the forest

chewy sap
oozing from
cracked bark

prickly balls
swaying on
long stems

I have picked
up your stars,
stuffed them
in a pocket,
let them burn
next to my heart

and gathered your
fruit to throw
at my enemies.

Pin Oak

I carried you
as a sapling
across the lawn

lower branches bending
earthward like a bundle
of divining rods
over a spring

set you in earth
near the septic tank

hosed summer water
through a tile
to your roots

and watched saucer-
shallow acorns
fall as brown
lobed leaves cleaved
into winter

heard my father
and his cronies
call you "piss oak"

left home, came
back and found
you taller than
the house in
which I grew up

your roots sucking
at the septic tank
so hard earth
bulged and buckled
around the base

stepped back
and stared at bark
closing around
the wound lightning
had gashed down
the middle
of your trunk.

Shagbark Hickory

Great strips
of patriarchal
bark peeling
off erect trunk

thin husks
splitting away
from hard shell
through which
squirrels, high
priests of the
forest, gnaw
for food

tough wood
from which my
fathers carved
tool handles,
barrel hoops,
wheel spokes
and gunstocks,
or burned to
smoke meat

I have stuffed
burlap bags
with your
fallen fruit

lugged them home
through the woods

and like a famished
fox squirrel
ground kernel
after kernel
between my teeth.

Chamomile

Along the border
of an Indiana garden
beside a cold frame

my great-grandparents
cultivated you for
the herb-blossom tea
they believed cured
most of their ills.

Oh calmer of nerves
and delirium tremens,
soother of headaches
and preventer of nightmares,
repeller of insects
and softener of hair

Oh spirit whose steamed
essence unclogged
my infected sinuses
in the Black Forest
and eased my eyelids
toward sleep

may your feathery
foliage and sunburst
flowers flourish in
the herb garden outside
the kitchen window.

Purple Trillium

Three petals,
three sepals,
three leaves.

Herb Trinity,
Trinity Lily,
Wake Robin,

your liver-red
flower blooms
when robins
return north.

Night Shade,
you love dank
humus and shadows
of trees.

Squaw Root,
Stinking Benjamin,

your maroon flower
gives off a fetor
to those who
come near.

My mother found
you instead of
"revenoors" when
she sneaked back
to the woods
behind the Indiana
farmhouse to stir
a kettle of cornmash.

Women have said
you help bring
on their monthly
flow of blood.

Birth Root,
you supposedly
ease the birth
of babes.

Trillium Erectum,
whose womanly flower
stands up on
a short stalk
above veined leaves,

stand straight
and stiff
in my garden.

In the name
of your petals
and sepals
and leaves
amen.

Tulip Poplar

You rise like
a classical column
above a ceiling
of secular leaves

gray bark
paling in grooves
around straight-
grained wood out
of which Indians
carved canoes

and my forefathers
framed an Indiana
homestead on a hill
and a courthouse
on the town square.

Your wide, four-
pointed leaves
notched at the tip
billow in the distance
like the sails
of immigrant ships.

                    *   *   *

I come to touch
the twin flames
of love and memory
of those who
came before
and disappeared
into the dark

to the delicate
candle that rises
out of a sac
of pollen

in the center
of your lime-
green tulip-
shaped flower.

Pawpaw

Ungainly sapling
everyone overlooks

leaves clumsy as
an overgrown athlete

in jest they
dub you
"the Hoosier banana."

As a boy I roamed
the hills of Dubois
County for the plump
fruit I found
a miraculous cross
between the yeoman
potato and the
noble banana.

I stood in thickets,
turned your flat
seeds with my tongue,
and sucked the juices
off those magic stones.

'Possums, squirrels,
raccoons and foxes
have the last laugh:

they gobble your
fruit before two-
legged animals
can touch it.

Persimmon

Patron of barren
woods and over-
grown fields

bark pocked
into squares
and rough diamonds

sparsely groomed
with toothless leaves

yet revisited like
a shrine by
almost every
bird and mammal

for the wrinkled
orange fruit
that puckered
my green mouth

but tickled my
ripe stomach
as a pudding.

Dutchman's Breeches

As if the
little Dutch boys
who wear you
at night

left you hang-
ing in pairs

in filtered sunlight
along this rotting
log on a hill

on an arching stalk

above delicately
divided pale
green leaves

white ankles up
yellow waist down

oh fragile
pantaloons

and had
so much fun

early this morning
they ran away

and never
came back.

Sugar Maple

You cluster like
domesticated animals
around southern
Indiana farmhouses

brown trunk ridged
like the hills
sloping toward Kentucky

five-lobed leaves,
velvet soft on
the underside,
sparking the flame
of October revolution.

I have awakened
to the blessing
of birdsong
in your branches

cupped your
winged fruit
in my hands

anointed my lips
with your sap.

Walnut

Loner, you stand
your own ground
as if to deepen
the mystery of
your darkness.

I have felt
the push of
your grain against
my shoulder in
the stock of
a double barrel
as I fired
into your limbs
blocking the sun.

As a boy
I filled gunny
sacks with your
lobed green fruit

hammered husks
against a brick

went to school
and hid stained
fingers beneath
a desk-top.

Now staring
into a refinished
veneer of your
earthen grain

I press a pencil
with pale fingers
back and forth
across papers

to conjure
your shadows.

Skinning a Rabbit

I rip off
bobtail
pull fur
down back
peeling it
over belly
yank it
over head
across paws
drop it on
old newspaper
insert knife
where naked legs
spread apart
slash down
through tender belly
as thin blood
drip drips
and guts bulge
stick hand
into slit
grab handfuls
of warm guts
which I tear
from back
chop head and paws
off with hatchet
plop whole wad
on top of fur
wrap corners
of newspaper
around bloody mess
compress it
into ball
to bury in garden
drop leftover flesh
in pail of water —

staring down
at a shrivelled
pink embryo
in reddening water
I blink to
the large streaking blur
my shotgun
blasted so still
and wonder why
I pulled the trigger
with such fever
the knife
with such relish
the guts
with such satisfaction.

Driving Back Roads Late at Night

Burrowing into the darkness
which bears down upon
the countryside like a mound
of dirt, my headlights uncover
furry bodies scattered
along narrow back roads.
Out of the corner of my eye
I catch glimpses of rabbits,
an occasional skunk, once
in a great while a stray tom
from a nearby farm — creatures
who were smacked from
the blind side by a bumper
or crushed beneath the tire
of someone who swerved too late,
slowed down momentarily
to recover from the thud,
and accelerated on his
dark course. After flinching
for several years when I began
to drive, now I too plow
straight ahead without much
hesitation into the darkness
which slides like dirt back
over the slumped bodies
as taillights glow red
in my rearview mirror.

Darkness Comes to the Woods

It begins to trickle
silently onto the floor
of the far side
of the woods which
the hunter cannot see.
First the creatures
dog-paddle in it, then
turn and float on their
backs as it creeps up
the bark of trees, pressing
down heavier and harder
on everything below.
Eventually the hunter
hears it lapping, then
breaking, then thundering
toward him. He turns
his back, splashes to
the field outside, looks
back on pairs of glowing
eyes gliding below
the surface of pitch-
black waters which have
swollen to the treetops.

Southern Indiana

And the hills roll
as they always have
and somewhere in the woods
that bend and wrap around
those hills the bark splits
from the trunk of a shagbark
hickory and a fox squirrel
drops a patter of cuttings
through crisp oversized leaves
as a boy with a shotgun
on his shoulder cocks ears
and trains eyes for a glimpse
of red fur between the parting
of green and at the edge
of the woods where dried
corn rustles in the breeze
Queen Anne's lace stands
in jagged profusion
and over these hills
that will always roll
a black chicken hawk
with eyes sharp for
the subtlest gradations
glides in a circle
that will never end.

Part Three:
CURVING BACK

Hoosier Songs

1

October sunlight
riding the ripples
of the Wabash
meandering southward
on my right

heart-shaped redbud
leaves burnished
to gold spindling
on the hillside
to my left

I glide like a sea gull
nearing the seashore
over sunlight and shade
streaking the surface
of winding River Road.

2

Heading due south
dead-center in the state
where I was born

I come home again
to these hills aglow
with October amber

and tall tulip
poplars billow
on the horizon

ivory-shafted
sycamores flutter
in the valleys

and clusters
of sugar maples
flicker and flare

as song rises
from the middle
of the heart.

St. Meinrad Archabbey

As I sit on a bench
beside the flagpole

on a hill of this remote
monastery in southern Indiana

a mockingbird sings a sliding
song within a holly tree.

This song would not seem
so loud and profane

but for the thick
silence surrounding us.

As whispered prayer seems
to push outward from cells

within sandstone buildings
his swiveling notes

fly outward from his
green cloister and glide

down the valley
shrouded in mist.

When he punctuates his
lyric with measured quiet

I conclude that native
song issuing from secluded

places is also one
essential kind of prayer.

To Obscure Men

This is a belated letter
to lonely old men like
the uncle who taught us
how to hunt, the neighbor
who took us on our first
camping trip, or the friend
of our father who organized
the excursion to our first
big-league ball game in
Cincinnati or St. Louis.
This is an inadequate,
belated letter to old men
everywhere who, after we
grew up, moved away from
the town, and never wrote
back, sustained themselves
for a few years on bitter-
sweet memories of laboring
in factories, sweating on
county road gangs, or working
the earth on hand-me-down
farms. . . . A long overdue,
unsuccessful letter to
unhappy old men who withered
away in parlors, hanged
themselves from two-by-four
rafters in garages, or shot
themselves in smokehouses
with the twelve gauges
they'd hunted with for fifty-
five years. . . . An impossibly
late but nevertheless contrite
letter from those of us
who have just grown old
enough to begin to remember.

Two Bricks and a Board

1

After years of moving
from one Franconian village
to another where they
worked other men's fields
as day laborers

after riding a bucking ship
across an untamed ocean
and coming inland
by railroad and riverboat
and walking north
along a corduroy road
into the wilderness
they found the right hill
south of the boundary between
Dubois and Spencer Counties.

They looked out over the valley
stretching to the east
and west and envisioned
ripe wheat and barley
rippling in the breezes
on the gentle slopes
and Indian corn taking
a stand in the bottoms.
They heard animals
grunting and cackling
in a barnyard at their back.

They took a long look,
said, *This is the place!*

They bought the land in 1853.
They felled poplars in the forest,
cut and hewed them into beams,
brought bricks from a kiln.
*

With their own peasant hands
and help from other German
immigrants who came out
of the woods they built their
own farmhouse on this hill
they had come so far to find.

2

Here they celebrated Elisabeth's
wedding to a young man from
another village in Lower Franconia.
Here my great-great-grandfather
Michael died in his bed after
deeding the farm to his son Johann.
Here my grandfather Benno was born
who one day walked across the valley
and crossed the county line
to the first farmhouse to the north
and asked my great-grandfather
August Luebbehusen for permission
to take his daughter Mary as his wife.

Here my father brought me
the year before he died to show
me the farmhouse his Uncle Alois
sold out of the family when
he moved to Missouri in 1911.

I stood on the creek-gravel
floor of the cellar, looked up
at a massive oak beam over my head,
stared at the wall three bricks thick.
I stood on the back porch and looked
down at the four-inch poplar saddle
of the doorway leading into the kitchen
worn at least an inch and a half
*

by the comings and goings
of so many generations. I stood
in the attic and squinted
at fourteen-inch poplar rafters
and thought of the strong hands
that had built this house.

3

I drive west along I-64,
as I always do when I come home,
and go one exit beyond my turn
so that I can see the brick
house again and ground myself.
I am home for the funeral
of the last uncle on my father's
side of the family, the brother
who was his business partner
over a quarter of a century.
More than ever before, I need
to witness the house on the hill.

I recognize the outer buildings
from a distance, but something
is wrong, terribly wrong.
Approaching the hill, I pull
off to the side of the interstate
as trucks roar past. I go
into shock, into a state of denial,
and pass beyond into a grief
you feel only when someone
close has died and you come
to understand you are powerless
to restore him or her to life.

Where the house they built
with their own hands
once stood is a huge
filled-in hole settling
like a fresh grave.

I learn the owners saved some
poplar beams for a new house,
set fire to what they could not use,
and bulldozed the burnt rubble
into a hole that was the cellar.

Friends of our family who live
nearby help me salvage something
to keep: two whitewashed bricks
and a jagged piece of poplar.

4

Blessed are the hands
that hewed this wood
and held these bricks.

Blessed are the names
of Michael, Johann,
and Elisabeth.

Blessed is the story
of their obscure lives
even though nobody
I know can tell me
anything about them.

Damned are those
who have no feeling
for the ones
who came before.

Damned are a people
who forget
as they move
relentlessly forward
into the progress
of the present
without preserving
at least a trace
*

of the lives
that built and shaped
the heritage
which shelters
and sustains them.

For to live
in the present
without remembering
the past is to
die a slow inhuman
death in a time
that leads nowhere
but back into
itself sealed off
forever from
life to come.

My Father Young Again

My father is young again
in the village of St. Henry,
Indiana that is somehow
no longer almost deserted.

Teamsters hauling freight
from the no-longer
defunct railroad station
in Johnsburg stop again

in the saloon of his
Prussian grandmother
that was torn down
and replaced by
a modern brick house

and they guzzle beer
and eat all they can
for a nickel and somehow
he is able to sleep
one more time the sleep
of the innocent
in the bedroom where
he was born above
the din of cardgames
and beery laughter.

As he grows older
he rides in the summer
beside his father
on the steam-engine
threshing machine that
has found its way back
into family hands
and cuts a neat swath
through golden-brown
wheat fields that roll
up and down hills.

➜

Evenings he walks
across the lane
into the shadows of
the small wooden church
built by the first German
settlers and watches
the flying squirrels
that have disappeared
glide from one tall
fir tree to another.

He quietly turns his
face and cries when
his father tells him
he must stop school after
the eighth grade because
the nearest high school
cannot be walked to and
they can't afford a horse.

So he guides a plow
behind his hotheaded
uncle's workhorse
for dirt-cheap wages
and room and board
and lessons in cursing

but he slips away again
on Saturday nights to
fiddle at barn dances
for a few bits and all
the beer he can drink.

Sunday afternoon he puts
on the cap and uniform
of the St. Henry Indians
and spins off the curve
and drop he's perfected
to the applause of spectators
assembled in the pasture

as the last rays of Sunday
sun filter through those
stained-glass windows
of the new village church
for which his father's
sawmill ripped for free
the timber cut from
his neighbors' woods —

in the very church where
I have cupped the sunlight
in my hands after it
flickered through family
names I have seen painted
in rectangles at the bottom
of those windows a short
walk from the cemetery
where familiar names
are carved in stone
in script row after row.

And now that my father
is dead he is still young
and growing younger and I
hold him there for my
children who have never
seen him except in pictures

and I safeguard him from
anxiety about the future
and the death of his
younger brother in World
War II and the nervous
breakdowns that robbed
him of speech, deprived
him of smiles and brought
him near a God he feared
would desert him at last

and I relieve him of
the fear that he would
never marry and know
the bittersweet joy
of raising four children

and I celebrate his perhaps
unwitting sense of irony
in marrying his brother's
former girlfriend who
like a frog in a folktale
turned into the mother
of the son who would
return to the land of his
youth and bring him back
to life once again.

A Terre Haute Story

It's the night before a wedding.
A table is set in Terre Haute, Indiana.
The last names of the bride and groom
begin with a K; both are solid German names.

The family of the groom is from the hills,
from the country. As small and backwoods
as it may seem to some, to them Terre Haute is
a big city. This dinner party is important.

The rented china and silver, fancy as can be,
glitter in all the artificial light. This
is a scene that might have been dramatized
in a novel by that German son of Terre Haute,

Theodore Dreiser, but you can be sure that
the parents of the groom never read novels.
If asked, the parents of the bride might
pretend to have read Dreiser of Terre Haute.

You must understand that the groom's folks
are country people who squirm when they enter
even a small-town restaurant for fear
of saying or doing the wrong thing.

They do not want to botch this affair.
The table is set, and the food is brought.
Maybe it's roast beef and mashed potatoes
and green beans or peas with a salad.

Whatever their social class, religion,
or profession, Americans of German descent
cannot resist good meat, good potatoes,
and even ordinary beer. Here in what

strikes them as a fancy house in Terre
Haute, Indiana, the night before a wedding,
champagne glasses have already been raised
to a toast by the father of the bride

and drained. As we all know, in our time
one in three marriages does not last. Much to
the eventual anguish of the parents of the groom,
this marriage will not last very long. . . .

Out of courtesy, the father of the bride,
who is Catholic in name only, turns to
the father of the groom, who is as Catholic
as German-Catholic can be, and asks if

he will please say a prayer before
the meal begins. The face of the father
of the groom turns almost as white
as his hair, he looks down at his

china plate, he tries to clear his throat
as if a catfish bone were stuck in it.
There is a painful silence in the big
house in Terre Haute, Indiana. Finally,

the mother of the groom begins to say,
"Bless us oh Lord and these thy gifts,"
and the meal can begin. And years later,
long after my father has died, my mother,

who has still not made peace with the divorce
of her second son, tells her eldest son
the secret of this story about the two German
families from southern Indiana: I knew

that half of each day of the eight and one-
half years that my father went to school was
conducted in German. I knew that my great-
grandfather had been born in Germany,

that my grandfather spoke mostly German,
that my father read and spoke German.
But I had not realized that my father
could speak to God only in German.

German Fries

An old man whose German name
means "little book" stands
at a gas stove in a house
in Jasper, Indiana.

The smell of onions sizzling
in bacon drippings between
slices of peppered potatoes
boiled in their skins
and chilled overnight
permeates the kitchen.

A wife who hobbles when
she walks sits in a rocker
near the table. Wife
and husband, mother
and father, seem sad.

Someone knocks on the door.
You can bet it's no one
terribly important, just
a neighbor come to deliver
a small bulging envelope.
The neighbor's German name
means "jelly-filled pastry"
and she seems even sadder
than the couple in the kitchen.

This woman hands the man
at the stove the envelope
and announces in a voice
too cheerful that donations
in the name of her late husband
for the Catholic charity
the two men had worked for
over several decades have
come to a good total.

You can believe it's not
fried onions alone
that bring tears to the eyes
of the man at the stove.
He will miss my father,
as his wife will; as my mother,
their neighbor, and we
four children will.

And as the smell of German fries
fills that kitchen in the hills
of southern Indiana to the level
of small lives deeply lived

no one knows that in a few years
the wife in the rocker will die
and several years after that
the soft-spoken son
of the old couple in the kitchen
who has lived most of his life
in a monastery on a hill
will become Bishop of Memphis
and later Archbishop of Indianapolis
and a few minutes before
being invested will quote
to a reporter some simple words
of warning impressed upon him
by the woman in the rocker:

*When you lead, don't ever think
you're better than those you lead.*

If you understand this simple
scene you know the Archbishop
of Indianapolis will never be able
to overcome his urge to eat
German fries in the kitchen.

Sisters

for Mary

My first sister
was born without
ever drawing a
breath. I heard
my mother cry
and my grandmother
scold her upstairs.

When my second sister
began to cry,
my mother breathed
a lot easier. My
grandmother smiled.
The dolls we kept
clapped their hands.

A Civil War Veteran from Indiana Recalls Visiting with Walt Whitman in a Washington Hospital

Even now, as I stare into the fire,
I can see him sitting there, that
lonely old man whose eyes fluttered
like quail roosting beyond the snowy
white bush of his whiskers and hair.
At first when I came to at dusk
and saw him sitting there, through
my fever, I was suspicious. As you
can imagine! What could an old man
want in a ward of wounded and dying
soldiers that reeked of gangrene
and piss? But when he spoke,
I relaxed. I had never heard
such a voice. His words were like salve
to my wound. He talked like one
of us, but somehow gentler.
He asked about my pain, if it was
better. I nodded. When I admitted
I was thirsty, he put water to my
lips. He wanted to know where my
folks lived, whether they'd heard
about my injury. When I shook
my head sideways and mumbled "Indiana,
southern Indiana," he said: "Oh, yes,
the hills. A Hoosier from the hills!"
He'd once sailed up the Ohio River
past Troy, he said, on his way back
from New Orleans. He wrote a letter
like I'd never read. It arrived like
balm for my mother's fears, beer
to my father's thirst for news. Mother
saved it till she died. "Don't worry,"
he wrote, "your brave son will be back
eating pawpaws soon." When I got back
enough strength to become a good listener,
*

he explained he'd gone all the way
from New York to Virginia looking
for his brother George; he'd been wounded
in the first Fredericksburg battle.
My God, how he loved to talk! Sometimes
I wondered who was the patient and who
was the aide. Outside the hospital
at Fredericksburg, he said, he found
"a heap of feet, arms, legs, and hands . . .
Enough to fill a whole horse cart!"
He shook his head, shuddered, and
sort of moaned: "And dead bodies
covered with brown woolen blankets."
He took a deep breath, then sighed:
"But George was alive and whole."
Sometimes when he looked into my eyes
from beyond that white bush, I thought
I might have once been his brother,
in some other world. I was by no means
the only soldier he visited. He'd come
into the ward coat and trouser pockets
bulging with gifts: apples, oranges,
sweet crackers, figs. Once he came
in carrying a jar of perserved raspberries
"donated by a lady." A few times I saw
him slip a coin into someone's moist
palm. Once I saw him lift a twist
of tobacco to an amputee's jaw.
Many's the time I watched him tear off
a sheet of paper from a pad, write
while he asked questions at the side
of the bed, and seal a letter into
an envelope. How that man loved
to write! To people from all over!
You'd have thought he was a parent himself.
*

He once confessed he'd written many
a tender love letter for the wounded.
That made him chuckle. The night before
I left, he read to me from a book.
I had never heard anything like it.
It was like the person in that book
was talking right to me, had known
me all my life. He spoke my kind
of language. It was beautiful without
being fancy. It was natural as sun,
rain, and snow. The rhythm swelled
like the sea, as I imagined it to sound.
I could see leaves of grass growing
on the graves of soldiers. I could
see a young boy growing up on an island
with an Indian-sounding name. I could
feel the sun on my shoulders, hear
the surf splash on the shore. When his
voice ebbed like that tide, I looked
into his soft eyes, and told him how
good it was. He smiled, thanked me,
said he wrote the book himself.
Watching the fire fade, I can still
hear his salty voice roll like the sea.

Theodore Dreiser's Cathedral

"Beyond [Huntingburg] was an equally fine road leading to Jasper,
the county seat. On this we encountered a beech grove so noble and
well planned that it had the sanctity and aroma of a great cathedral."
—Theodore Dreiser, *A Hoosier Holiday* (1916)

After thirty years, you return
to the Hoosier state for a holiday.
After revisiting Evansville,
on the Ohio, you and your Hoosier
artist friend drive north
along wretched roads toward
Bloomington and the University
where you spent a year standing
in the dark in the bushes aching
for the daughter of a professor.

In the bottom land where puddles
and streams block the way,
a bridge collapses and sinks
just after you reach the far end.

Ach Theodor, you eternal outsider,
always aroused, always moving on,
always yearning for the glow of light
from another quarter, another life,
always striking out for the home
that escapes you like the father
who wandered from town to town
in search of the job that would
finally support the brood of ten.

Where you really want to go,
Theodore, is French Lick,
a name to tempt and arouse
any German boy from the hills
of southern Indiana. Where
big brother Paul, famous songwriter,
modern Falstaff who "roystered
with drinkers and women," went
for his licks and kicks.

➙

And so on your way toward
the resort for the rich
sequestered in the hills you
and your New York artist-chauffeur
from Indiana have to pass
through the German-Catholic town
where I was born and grew up.

You fellow Hoosier German,
my father was but a teenager
in a nearby village well off
the main road when you motored
through godforsaken towns where
hicks gawked at the fancy car
from the East and horses and dogs
scattered at the blare of the horn.

It was the car, Ted, and not
the novelist, that fascinated
the folk! Surely they had
never heard of the controversial
Sister Carrie, that fascinating
tale in which you poured yourself
into your outsider sisters
and made it big in the big city
as a fictional projection while
managing to remain miserable
as both a character and person.

You and your Missouri wife Jug
could never make a go of it,
but she would never let go;
and so you shared your misery
and some good moments with
an attractive distant cousin,
Helen, who one day knocked at your
New York City novelist's door.
She had been reading your books. . . .

When you and Franklin enter
Dubois County, named after a French
Indian fighter but settled by
Baden and Bavarian immigrants,
you begin to feel better about your
southern Indiana origins. As poor
homes, poor stores, and puny farms
recede in the rearview mirror,
your German spirit soars. Perhaps
you can now begin to forget about
the poverty-stricken childhood.

Near Holland, where the nearest
high school was located, too far
away for my father to walk to
from St. Henry and inaccessible to
a family too poor to afford a horse,
you find a splendid wide road.
You and Franklin "tear along."

Huntingburg, so "alive and clean,"
you like, you Deutscher! The houses
are well built, the streets nice
and wide, the stores attractive.
A would-be burgher, you admire
the "brisk businesslike atmosphere."

Ted, my brother of sorts, I must
confess we Jasper German-Catholics
hated Huntingburg with a senseless
passion, no matter how clean
or prosperous it was. They were
German Protestants, and, even worse,
they too were damned good in basketball!

Heading north toward my hometown
along that treacherous winding
road in the bottom land that we
teenagers tore along, passing
*

one another on blind curves,
with steep banks and swamp water
on either side, racing to
the ultimate religious rite,
a basketball game in the domain
of our archrivals, you Hoosier
German mystic masquerading as
a New York City skeptic,
you have a spiritual experience.

Not far from where my grandfather
ripped with his steam-engine sawmill
into the great trunks of trees he told
my father could never be replaced,
you find a beech grove so noble
"and well planned it has the aroma
of a great cathedral." Like
any German skeptic with a soft
romantic center, you follow
your nose, leave the motorcar,
and worship in singular fashion
the gods you always rebel against.
While Franklin does a drawing
of "A Cathedral of Trees,"
you put your arms behind your back
and gaze aloft into the silvery
branches as to the West the sun,
a great red ball of fire, sinks
between the great beech columns.

You lay hands on their silvery smooth
trunks and then on your cheeks.
You almost ask them to bless you,
you say, to help you grow strong,
to help you grow natural and frank.

As your German ancestors must
have done once upon a time,
you look into the pools of swamp
*

water and ask all wood nymphs
and water sprites to one day
admit you into their
happy councils and revels.

Your ritual accomplished,
your Teutonic spirits uplifted,
you proceed into the county seat,
Jasper, where you "heartily approve"
of the new courthouse set on
a slight incline so that it
commands the eye from all
four approaches, and St. Joseph's
sandstone church, "a triumph of taste."

If it hadn't been so late, you admit,
you would have gone for the key.
No doubt you would have worshipped
the stately columns, each a gigantic
tulip poplar from the local forest,
and implored the wood nymphs
and water sprites to bless you
and admit you into the ceremony.

Your fanatically Catholic father
should have worshipped here
with my relatives, renegade Ted.
We are a God-fearing, hardworking
people, my fellow Hoosier German.
Your father should have come here to work
in one of the wood factories. Like my
father, he could have built chairs.
His big brood of Kinder could have
gone to school under the good nuns
missionary Rev. Joseph Kundek of Croatia
recruited from your native Terre Haute,
from "Our-Lady-of-the-Woods."

"What a charming place in which
to grow up!" you think.

→

Yes, Ted, you could have served
mass while your father sat praying
next to one of the poplar columns.
You could have drunk beer and whiskey
on Saturday nights at a local
dance hall and thrown up your
frustrations in the parking lot.
You could have stood on a sidewalk
outside the brick house of one
of the factory owners and lusted
for the blonde doing her homework
at the oak table in the kitchen.
You could have learned to throw
a ball through a hoop and become
a local legend, then died shortly
after high school when the applause
faded and there was no place to go
for the son of an immigrant,
except perhaps very far away.

My Hoosier cousin, I leave you
in my hometown to daydream
of the spring waters, the gaudy hotel,
and the pleasures your big brother
had savored in French Lick.

I leave you to admire "the machines
of the best make and parties
of well-to-do people" you observe
around the elevated Court House
in Jasper, Dubois County, Indiana.

I leave you there to cruise
into the "moonlit hills"
where you may find yet another
cathedral and aroma enough
to inspire even you to worship.

Flight

The onset of adolescence
flushes fidgeting children
like coveys of quail
from brooding parents.

The children fly in formation
over neighborhood fences
toward foreign fields
and light separately

in exotic bushes, but as
soon as they tire of
cramming their craws
with novel berries and seeds

they come winging back
in pairs feeling deep
in their beaks a need
to peck familiar grain.

Boy Scouts Camping Out

We sat cross-legged peering into the fire
with a circle of tents at our back.

Flickering coals spotlighted the face
of the scout whose turn it was to talk.

Sucking on cigarettes, we voted on who
was the raunchiest girl in our class,

then swore on a rusty Swiss Army knife
that none of us would ever get hitched.

We wondered about our mothers and fathers
and swapped notes on our budding sisters.

By the time the sunlight began to trickle
through the treetops, we crawled back into

our tents coughing like cranes and fell
with swollen imaginations into heavy sleep.

The Patoka River and the Blessinger Brothers

*Wolf, how deep is
the water*, it meant
in the Miami tongue.

Deep enough to swallow
the two Blessinger
brothers one Sunday.

Neighborhood play
broke apart that afternoon
when the phone call

to a relative brought
the news we could not
even begin to accept.

The sky drew as tight
as skin over pus
about to pop

as we waited for
an eyewitness account.
Finally, the carload

of relatives and friends
and the hurried story
in hushed voices:

Jim, the tall quiet
softball player with
those deft hands,

dragged up from the river
bottom, flesh clammy white,
carried away on a stretcher;

Charlie, "Chas," the short
peppery basketball player
with springy legs and hands

stained brown every fall
from dehusking walnuts,
dragged up from the river

bottom, foam bubbling
from his nostrils.
For years I stared across

the classroom at their
silent brother Ron, thought
of my two brothers, never

knew what to say:
Too deep, Patoka,
too deep for words.

For an Old Friend

What a cruel way to learn
the news! The hometown newspaper,
arriving well after the fact,
tactfully placed your picture
and story on the second page.
I almost overlooked it that late
Friday afternoon when I settled in,
tired, for the weekend. The same
fine features I remember from ten
years ago, the look of the hometown
boy destined to go far, very far.
But, for whatever reasons, you
came back home from New York.
You came back to the town you
once loved, but could no longer
accommodate your needs, couldn't
even give you the simple urge
to keep on breathing. You were
drinking heavily, I hear. Last
time I saw you, at the town library,
you appeared on the street with
a flushed face, said hello, offered
a nervous hand, hurried back home
through the alley. I still cannot
believe what I read. I cannot
accept the idea of you hanging
from a belt in the bedroom.
I want to sing you back out
of the darkness, onto your feet.
I want to release the tension
around your throat and sing
the breath of life back into
your lungs, hear that whiplash
wit, listen to deaf Beethoven's
ecstatic last symphony as we
sip from mugs of beer, argue
American literature, discuss
the merits of various cuisines.
But it's no use, Jeff. The poem
is always too much after the fact.

Basketball Season Begins

Except for the throng
buzzing in the gymnasium,
the town might seem deserted.
Tonight no one drives
up or down Main Street.
Soon every factory worker
balanced on the edge
of the bleachers will
know as exactly as his
boss leaning back in his
chair seat how each of these
high-school athletes measures
up against the heroic
individuals on that yardstick
championship team. Every gas
station attendant will be able
to decree as authoritatively
as the superintendent of schools
at what point the new coach's
back deserves to be patted
or his throat summarily slit.
On Monday morning, mayor
and minister alike will inform
their followers exactly why
this team will sputter or soar.
Every native wedged into
this sweaty brick building
has wagered his small-town
heritage on the outcome
of this season. The town
has lain dormant for many
a month; at the opening tip-
off it roars itself awake.

Hills

1

Out of the mist
gentle hills emerge.

Woods and trees rounded,
fields ripe and bounded.

All is focused and full.
Only I seem to move.

Gold and crimson,
yellow and burnt sienna
blend with green

subdued and settled
in the rising mist.

2

A cricket grates
a steady song
on the middle floor
of the archabbey library

where I peer
through a magnifying glass
at archaic German script
and move my lips.

A gentle landscape
breeds a quiet song.

3

I look out over
the valley to the gym
where I played
grade-school basketball.

I sink another long
two-handed set shot,
even then well behind
the fashion of the day.   ➜

The cord net rustles
after the clean swish.

A soft touch,
a quiet voice.

Curving Back

I

A hayseed ballplayer stands
self-consciously in full uniform
before the trunk of a huge tree
girdled with vines. He wants
to grin at the camera
but clamps his mouth shut
over a brace of buckteeth.
A tight unlettered cap shades
his eyes. Boldface lettering
across his chest proclaims
the team: INDIANS. It doesn't
say so, but the place is St. Henry,
Indiana. This is the 1920s.

The buckle of his wide leather
belt is way off center, the stubby
glove on his left hand flopping
against baggy pinstripes
couldn't hold a bunch of prunes.
The woolen socks that itch
at the knees begin with a band
of red and open into an expanse
of white swallowed by a pair
of high-topped clodhopper
spikes that dig into pasture
turf with a sharp bite.

The nose is mine. The ballplayer
with the wicked curve is my father.
It's time for him to turn around
and warm up for the Sunday afternoon
game on the diamond laid out
on the other side of the tree.

II

Now it's the early 1950s
and a boy and his father face
one another at the edge
of a woods in Sunset Terrace
just outside Jasper, Indiana.
Their left hands snuggle
into folds of padded leather.
The boy grips the baseball along
the seams, winds up, tries to
snap the ball as he releases
it so it breaks just as his
father has promised him it
one day will. As the ball
spins and curves ever so
slightly, the boy grins.
The father nods as the ball
smacks his padded palm.

After supper they drive
to the town ballpark to watch
the Jasper Reds play another
semipro team from southern Indiana,
under the lights. The ballplayers,
many of them relatives, chatter
with German accents. The father,
his knee shattered in a wreck,
holds the boy's hand as they climb
the bleachers for a good seat.
Toward the end of the game,
the hometeam behind, the slugger
finally connects with men on base.
The father, the son, all their
friends leap to their feet.

The ball rises and rises,
it heads toward rows of lights
perched atop a wooden pole

higher than the tallest tree
in the forest, it keeps rising
and clears those bright lights
soaring above and beyond.
That white pill of a ball
spins in a beautiful trajectory,
from past toward present. It
will never come back to earth.

III

Now it's the late 1970s
and the father is retired.
The son has flown home from
New York for a visit. Once again
the fresh-cut grass smells
of wild onion and they decide
to watch the high-school baseball
team play in the state tournament.
The father, hobbling, negotiates
steps and bleachers as poorly
as he does his retirement.
He lets his son grasp his hand
and guide him to a good seat.

Memories of games under these
lights drift past like pollen,
but neither wants to speak.
Today the ball will not leap off
the new aluminum bats as it
once did off solid ash.
The young players can't put
the ball into orbit. Sadness
falls upon the bleachers. This
is the father's last season.

➜

IV

Now it's the mid 1980s.
A father, his wife, daughter
and son walk into a stadium
in the bombed-out Bronx.
In a landscape of cracked concrete,
broken glass, and rubble,
the playing field is a magic
mix of emerald grass, sunshine,
and blue sky. As the players
warm up, the father thinks
of the young man in the hayseed
uniform of the St. Henry Indians.
These big-city big-league pinstripes
are chic, but one player dares to
wear his stockings in the old style.

This ballplayer is from southern
Indiana, from a German town
on the Ohio River. You can tell
he loves the game with a fervor.
His swing is pure grace.
He digs in his cleats, takes
practice swings for his first
at bat, bears down hard.
The pitcher releases a ball
that curves in toward the batter
but hangs at the waist.

He unleashes an almost level
swing that sends the ball
rising on a line toward
right field. Everyone stands,
cheers: the ball is frozen
in flight as it heads toward
the far reaches of a green
pasture in St. Henry, the lights
above Recreation Field in Jasper,
the Ohio River in Evansville.

I cup my hands to catch this
ball that may never land so
I can carry it home and spin
the seams to send it curving
on in memory that is sacred.

Somewhere in Southern Indiana

Somewhere in southern Indiana
a boy sits listening to a baseball game
on the radio. It is very quiet
in the house where his mother sits
darning socks and his father flips
through a seed catalogue. The dark
wooded hills surround the house,
which is far removed from city lights
and baseball games. The only sounds
outside are the barking of a neighbor's
dog down the road and, occasionally,
the crunching of pickup tires over rocks.

This boy who listens to the baseball
game never reads poetry, except when
he is required to for his English class.
He would not be interested in what
I write. He thinks poetry must be about
English knights and ladies in castles,
not boys who listen to baseball games,
mothers who darn socks, fathers who
look through seed catalogues.

One day the boy will move away
from southern Indiana to a big city
where he will go to fine restaurants
and concerts and plays and begin to
read poetry on his own. He will feel
something stir within, and he will go
to the library, browse through magazines
in the periodicals room, pull off volumes
of poems from the stacks, and take them
home to his apartment. He will feel
a thumping in his chest, take out a piece
of paper, and try to make a poem.

Every sentence he begins will pull him
back to a scene in which a boy
sits listening to a baseball game
*

on the radio, a mother sits darning
socks, a father sits flipping through
a seed catalogue. The longer he
listens to the thumping within,
the louder he will hear the barking
of a dog and the crunching
of pickup tires over rocks.

Norbert Krapf was born in the German community of Jasper, Indiana, in 1943. He holds degrees from St. Joseph's College (Indiana) and the University of Notre Dame. His poems have appeared in more than a hundred magazines and anthologies and have been collected in eight limited editions, including *A Dream of Plum Blossoms* and *Lines Drawn from Dürer*. He has edited an anthology of writings by contemporary poets about William Cullen Bryant and translated collections of the poetry of Rainer Maria Rilke and legends from his ancestral Franconia. He is completing an expansion of a collection of pioneer German journals and letters from his native Dubois County, *Finding the Grain*. Since 1970, he has taught English at the C.W. Post Campus of Long Island University.

Also available from
Time Being Books

LOUIS DANIEL BRODSKY
You Can't Go Back, Exactly
The Thorough Earth
Four and Twenty Blackbirds Soaring
Mississippi Vistas: Volume One of *A Mississippi Trilogy*
Forever, for Now: Poems for a Later Love
Mistress Mississippi: Volume Three of *A Mississippi Trilogy*
A Gleam in the Eye: Poems for a First Baby
Gestapo Crows: Holocaust Poems

LOUIS DANIEL BRODSKY and WILLIAM HEYEN
Falling from Heaven: Holocaust Poems of a Jew and a Gentile

ROBERT HAMBLIN
From the Ground Up: Poems of One Southerner's Passage
to Adulthood

WILLIAM HEYEN
Erika: Poems of the Holocaust
Pterodactyl Rose: Poems of Ecology
Ribbons: The Gulf War — A Poem

RODGER KAMENETZ
The Missing Jew: New and Selected Poems

JOSEPH MEREDITH
Hunter's Moon: Poems from Boyhood to Manhood

10411 Clayton Road • Suites 201-203
St. Louis, Missouri 63131
(314) 432-1771

TO ORDER TOLL-FREE
(800) 331-6605 Monday through Friday, 8 a.m. to 4 p.m. Central time
FAX: (314) 432-7939

Please call or write for a free catalog.